DATE DUE

HIGHSMITH #45230

Printed
in USA

Feeling Shy

For a free color catalog describing Gareth Stevens' list of high-quality books and multimedia programs, call 1-800-542-2595 (USA) or 1-800-461-9120 (Canada). Gareth Stevens Publishing's Fax: (414) 225-0377.
See our catalog, too, on the World Wide Web: http://gsinc.com

The author and original publisher would like to thank the staff and pupils of the following schools for their help in the making of this book: St. Barnabas Church of England Primary School, Pimlico; Kenmont Primary School, Hammersmith & Fulham; St. Vincent de Paul Roman Catholic School, Westminster; Mayfield Primary School, Cambridge; St. Peter's Church of England Primary School, Sible Hedingham.

Library of Congress Cataloging-in-Publication Data

Althea.
    Feeling shy / by Althea Braithwaite; photographs by Charlie Best; illustrations by Conny Jude.
        p. cm. — (Exploring emotions)
    Includes bibliographical references and index.
    Summary: Examines the nature of shyness, what can cause it, and how to deal with it.
    ISBN 0-8368-2119-X (lib. bdg.)
    1. Bashfulness in children—Juvenile literature. [1. Bashfulness.]
I. Best, Charlie, ill. II. Jude, Conny, ill. III. Title. IV. Series: Althea. Exploring emotions.
BF723.B3A57   1998
155.2'32—dc21   98-5585

This North American edition first published in 1998 by
Gareth Stevens Publishing
1555 North RiverCenter Drive, Suite 201
Milwaukee, Wisconsin 53212 USA

Series consultant: Dr. Dorothy Rowe

Gareth Stevens series editor: Dorothy L. Gibbs
Editorial assistant: Diane Laska

Printed in Mexico

1 2 3 4 5 6 7 8 9 02 01 00 99 98

Exploring Emotions

Feeling Shy

Althea

Photographs by
Charlie Best

Illustrations by
Conny Jude

Gareth Stevens Publishing
MILWAUKEE

Do you ever feel shy?

I feel shy when I meet someone new.

Meeting my parents' friends makes me feel shy.

4

- Going to new places
- Asking a question in class
- Going to parties where you hardly know anyone
- Meeting someone for the first time

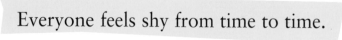
Everyone feels shy from time to time.

5

How does shyness make you feel?

People show their shyness in different ways.

I get a stomachache.

I feel hot all over.

Feeling shy is not wrong — and you don't have to find a cure. You will feel better, however, if you learn how to cope with shyness in different situations.

Janet deals with her shyness about meeting new people by trying to ask questions that will start a conversation.

Have you read this book? It's great!

Janet says, "If I start talking about something interesting, I get really involved, and I forget I felt shy in the first place."

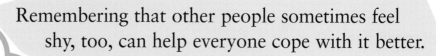

Remembering that other people sometimes feel shy, too, can help everyone cope with it better.

Samantha felt very nervous when she started attending a new school. She had just moved with her mom and dad, and she had to say goodbye to all her friends.

Everyone has friends except me.

At lunchtime, Rashida saw Samantha looking a little lost.

"I felt shy because I didn't know Samantha, but I could see that she didn't know where to sit. So I waved to her."

You can sit over here!

"Samantha was glad I asked her over. We started talking, and now we're good friends."

11

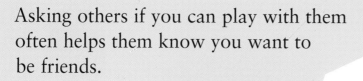

Asking others if you can play with them often helps them know you want to be friends.

It's not always easy to do.

I feel funny about asking to play with them right away.

At times, waiting a while to ask is a good idea. It gives you a chance to watch what the others are doing and learn the rules of the game, which makes joining in easier later on.

12

If you don't ask to join in, other people might think it's because you don't want to be friends with them. Sometimes, the people you ask won't let you join them. Don't worry. You probably wouldn't enjoy being with them anyway. You can always ask someone else — when you feel ready.

13

Some people feel shy when they're asked to speak in front of others.

Rebecca says, "I always raise my hand in class, but when the teacher calls on me, my face starts to feel hot, and I forget what I was going to say."

Rebecca's teacher calls on someone else to give Rebecca time to think. Later on, when she is ready, Rebecca says what she wanted to say.

I found this shell on the beach!

Rebecca was happy that she managed to tell the others about the shell she found.

She says, "I thought, again, about what I wanted to say. Then, when I felt ready, I raised my hand."

15

When you have something difficult to say, you might feel very awkward and shy. Telling your parents or a teacher about something that is worrying you can take a lot of courage.

When Matt finally manages to tell his mom about a problem, she listens carefully and is very helpful.

Mom, I want to tell you something, but I'm afraid you'll laugh at me.

Adults don't always listen carefully. Try to talk to them at a time when you know they can give you their full attention.

Do you ever feel shy about saying or doing something different? Perhaps you are worried that other people will laugh at you for it.

Rashida says, "I felt very shy when I told my family I didn't want to eat meat anymore. No one else in our house is a vegetarian.

When I told some friends at school how I felt, a lot of them agreed with me."

When you say how you feel, you often will find that other people feel the same way.

I think it's wrong to kill animals.

People sometimes tease others who look or act different in some way. Being teased can make people feel angry or shy.

Craig says, "I get teased at school about the clothes my mom buys me."

Craig has learned to laugh about it and tease back. "That way, I don't mind being teased so much myself."

When people tease us, it doesn't necessarily mean they don't like us. It can help to laugh about it and maybe even tease them back.

She always buys me clothes that are too big!

19

Sometimes, adults can make you feel shy. Kate says, "When we visit Uncle Josh, the people in his family all stand around together talking loudly and laughing at everything."

Sometimes, they ask me questions, but I never really know what to say.

"Mom tells me not to worry; they make her feel shy, too. She says I should write them a thank-you note to show that I care about them, even though I'm always so quiet at their parties."

You might feel shy about singing, acting, or even talking in front of other people. Adults don't always understand why. They worry that you are not enjoying yourself.

Janek says, "I always hated going to parties. I felt silly playing the games. Now I get out of playing the games by helping to organize them instead."

Do some situations make you feel especially awkward? Can you think of ways to change these situations so you will feel more comfortable?

Rebecca was embarrassed when her dad came to her school one day. Her friends told her that their parents made them feel embarrassed or shy at times, too. We have to learn to accept that everyone is different. We can't expect people to change just so they don't embarrass us.

His clothes are all wrong. Everyone will laugh!

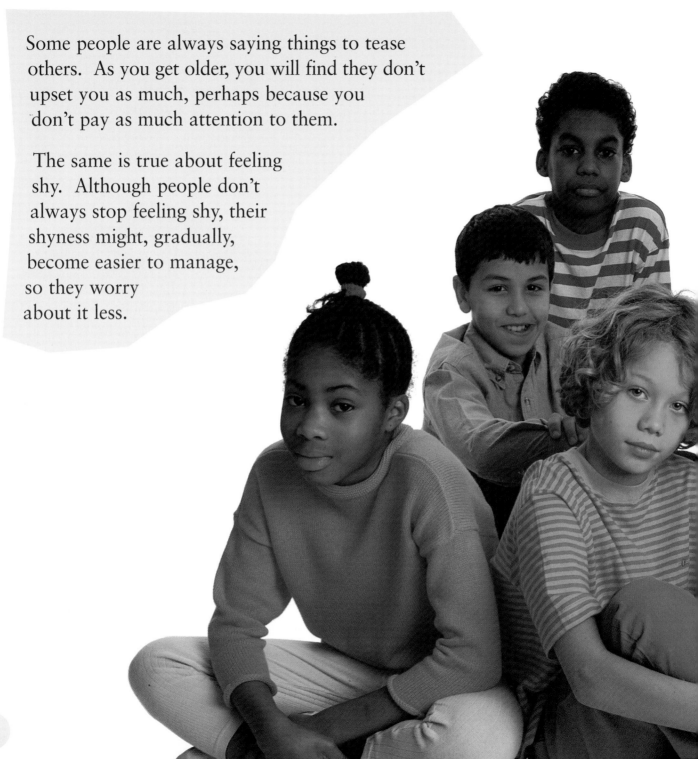

Some people are always saying things to tease others. As you get older, you will find they don't upset you as much, perhaps because you don't pay as much attention to them.

The same is true about feeling shy. Although people don't always stop feeling shy, their shyness might, gradually, become easier to manage, so they worry about it less.

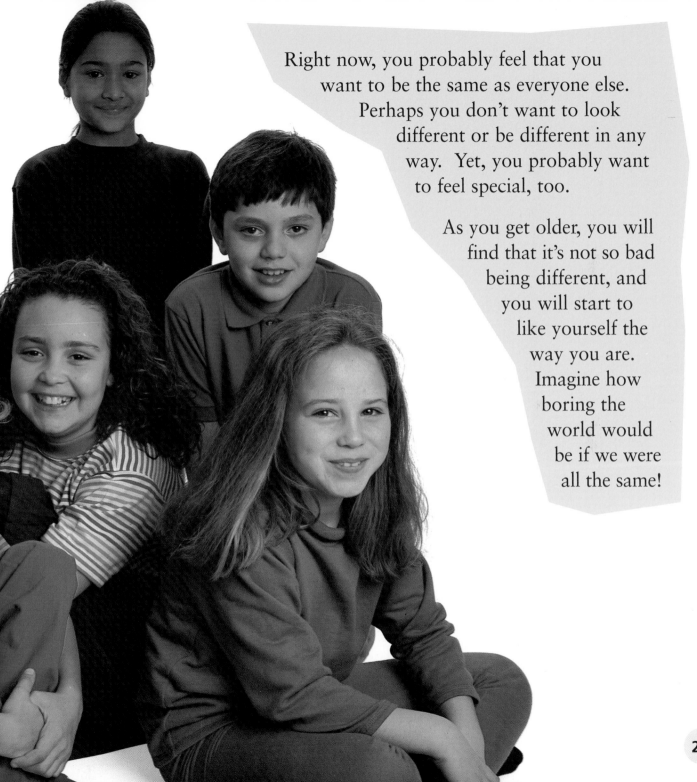

Right now, you probably feel that you want to be the same as everyone else. Perhaps you don't want to look different or be different in any way. Yet, you probably want to feel special, too.

As you get older, you will find that it's not so bad being different, and you will start to like yourself the way you are. Imagine how boring the world would be if we were all the same!

For Teachers and Parents
A Note from Dorothy Rowe

We all feel shy at times, not because of what happens to us, but because of how we feel about what happens to us. Teachers and parents know that children need help understanding and dealing with feelings of shyness. Adults sometimes forget, however, that, in order to help, they first must know both the child's situation and how he or she feels about it.

A child won't see a situation the same way an adult does for the simple reason that no two people, whatever their ages, ever see things in exactly the same way. An adult shouldn't assume he or she knows what's wrong with a child, but, rather, should explore possible reasons for the child's shyness by seeking answers to questions like: "Is this child shy because he or she is frightened of other children?" or "Is this child shy because he or she has had some bad experiences and doesn't want to get hurt again?"

Dozens of reasons are possible answers to the question, "Why does this child behave this way?" Thinking of these alternatives helps the adult ask better questions. The answers, however, can come only from the child.

Feeling shy isn't a problem that can be solved once and for all. It is a dilemma we face all our lives. There is no cure for feeling shy; people just have to find ways to cope with shyness. Adults must be prepared to share with children their own experiences, including the difficulties they have had coping with shyness. They should not pretend to provide easy solutions to overcoming shyness. This way, adults and children can explore the shyness dilemma together.

Suggestions for Discussion

To start a discussion and get everyone involved, you and the children could write lists of all the things that make you feel shy. Then, compare lists. As an alternative, you could have the children help you compile a single list of specific situations that can cause shyness. Then, have them rate each situation in terms of whether it makes them feel "very shy," "a little shy," or "not shy at all."

Examples of situations that make people feel shy include:

- Walking into a room full of people you don't know.

- Speaking in front of the class.

- Talking to grown-ups about your problems.

Encourage the children to be honest with their answers. Even many adults feel shy when they have to speak to a group or talk about their problems.

Many of the reasons for shyness and the ways to cope with it can be discussed with children while going through this book, page by page. The following points might help start your discussions.

Page 7
If you don't look at people when they speak to you, or when you speak to them, they might think it's because you don't like them.

Pages 8-9
Being friendly to new people is more important than worrying about what to say to them.

Pages 10-11
People often feel shy in new situations, because they don't know what will happen from one minute to the next.

Pages 12-13
Sometimes, the people you are shy around are just as shy around you. If you are a new person, they don't know what to expect from you any more than you know what to expect from them.

Page 16
Problems are not the only things children are shy about sharing. They also might feel shy about telling people something interesting they have learned, or something exciting that has happened to them.

Page 17
Sometimes, people are shy about saying how they feel because they think others will laugh at them.

Pages 18-19
People often tease others because they want to get to know them, but they aren't sure what to say to them. Laughing with people is a good way to let them know you'd like to be friends.

Pages 20-21
An adult might ask questions that seem silly or confusing to a child, because adults don't always know what to say to children. They often feel shy around them, even though they try to act like they're not. Because the questions adults ask are sometimes difficult to answer without sounding vague or impolite, the child feels shy, too.

Page 23
People who feel embarrassed by someone else sometimes try to apologize for or explain the other person and end up calling attention to things that others probably hadn't even noticed.

Page 24
Some people will always feel shy in certain situations, but, as they get older and more experienced, most of them find ways to look, and even feel, less shy in order to succeed in jobs and in social relationships. Some children might already have stories to share about how they are starting to "outgrow" shyness.

Page 25
Although children might tease other children who look or act differently, they often are very interested in getting to know those children better. They might even secretly wish to be more like those children or to be less shy about looking or acting differently themselves.

More Books to Read

Being Me. Life Education (series).
  Alex Parsons (Watts)

Emotional Ups and Downs.
  Good Health Guides (series).
  Enid Fisher (Gareth Stevens)

Help for Kids: Understanding
  Your Feelings about Moving.
  Carole Gesme and Larry Peterson
  (Pine Tree Press)

If Only. . . A Story about Self-
  Acceptance for Grades 1-5.
  Lori Rigberg (Mar Co Products)

If You Had to Choose, What Would
  You Do? Sandra M. Humphrey
  (Prometheus Books)

Why Do Kids Need Feelings?
  A Guide to Healthy Emotions.
  Monte Elchoness (Monroe Press)

Videos to Watch

How I Learned Not To Be Bullied.
  (Sunburst Communications)

Learning to Say How You Feel.
  (Sunburst Communications)

Lessons from the Heart (series).
  (United Learning, Inc.)

No More Teasing!
  (Sunburst Communications)

Web Sites to Visit

www.pbs.org/adventures/

KidsHealth.org/kid/feeling/

Due to the dynamic nature of the Internet, some web sites stay current longer than others. To find additional web sites, use a reliable search engine with one or more of the following keywords to help you locate information about feeling shy. Keywords: *bashful, behavior, emotions, feelings, introvert, self-conscious, shy.*

Glossary

attention — the act of focusing your thoughts and activities on the needs and wants of someone or something that interests you.

awkward — acting or feeling clumsy or embarrassed; not showing the skill, grace, or confidence required in a particular situation.

boring — not interesting; dull.

comfortable — feeling good, relaxed, or safe, physically or emotionally.

conversation — the act of two or more people exchanging information, thoughts, and ideas verbally with each other; an informal discussion.

cope — to deal with, or overcome, a problem or a difficult situation.

courage — strength of mind and emotions to face danger, fears, or serious difficulties.

embarrassed — feeling uncomfortable, upset, or self-conscious in a situation because of what others might think or say about you.

involved — very interested in or busy with someone or something.

join — to come together with another individual or to become part of a group.

natural — looking or acting the way nature originally designed; not fake, pretend, or exaggerated.

nervous — jumpy, uneasy, unsteady.

shy — tending to withdraw or stay away from other people.

tease — to annoy or irritate someone in a mischievous way.

vegetarian — a person who eats only foods that come from plants, does not eat meat, but might, sometimes, eat eggs and dairy products.

Index